# THE TRAIL IN THE WOODS

## A GIFT OF WISDOM TO SONS AS THEY
## TRAVEL THE WOODS OF THIS LIFE

### MICHAEL BRANDON WILLIAMS

ISBN 978-1-0980-1416-2 (paperback)
ISBN 978-1-0980-1417-9 (digital)

Christian Faith Publishing, Inc.
832 Park Avenue
Meadville, PA 16335
www.christianfaithpublishing.com

Printed in the United States of America

To Hunter Dane and Drayton Reed,

Every dad wants his failings to be stepping-stones for his sons.
I love you bigger than words. Keep stepping and trusting in Him.
I'll be at the tree.

Dad

# *Acknowledgements*

*ALL HAIL KING JESUS*

# *Contents*

# *Foreword*

"So I'm a man now?" I recall the internal question on my nineteenth birthday. I didn't understand what expectation came with being "a man", but I knew things would change. Truth is the process of becoming a man (it never ends) can be confusing. The world tells us that we can only be accepted by conforming to the mold (what we own, what we can create) while our very nature cries out for adventure, a journey...a battle. Whether it is in a good war movie, a western or a fantasy like *Lord of the Rings, Gladiator* or *Braveheart*—we long to be a part of something fought for. The truth is we do have battles but ours are often less cinematic and can be hidden in the everyday—an ever-winding journey into the woods. But who can direct us? Why would we trust them? What if I don't want to "live and learn" but to "learn and live?" Can I get wisdom without all the wounds that often accompany it?

As a young man, I found that even the greatest of wisdom can be hard to receive. Ironically, as an older man, I have found it equally difficult to impart. You can feel inadequate and recall your own resistance to wise counsel. I remember wisdom being boring, almost suffocating, so I endured and often refused these riches from great men who had no reason to lie to me. I've had mentors like World War II veterans who stormed the beaches of Normandy to missionaries who have seen God's angels protect them. Wisdom has been imparted from elders of the church who have witnessed both the miraculous and the mundane in generations of believers. I have heard from broken men who have received all the riches they could from this world, and yet remained empty, to those who owned almost nothing but shared everything in joy. From the heroic to the homeless, I heard them but seldom truly listened. *Why?*

Jesus spoke in parables, David in song, and Solomon in proverbs because God knows the minds of men. Although "discovery learning" became all the rage in education back in the '60s, God knew long ago how men preferred to learn. We can fall asleep at the most inopportune times and miss the very treasure we live to see (Matthew 26: 40–45). But we love to hunt, to explore...thus God lets us "seek" (Matthew 6:33) so that we may find. Whether a riddle, a puzzle or a mystery...we just love to discover hidden things—the greatest discovery, the greatest gift.

When wisdom is imparted, it may be one of the purest forms of masculine love. Solomon (whose "*wisdom and riches exceeded all others*" [1 Kings 10:23]) set the pursuit of wisdom as one of man's highest callings. So he shared it. I now know that sharing wisdom is love but accepting or refusing love is a choice. Our mind is enticed when we must engage, search it out...to hunt it. As Solomon wrote, "*It is the glory of God to conceal a matter; to search out a matter is the glory of kings*" (Prov. 25:2).

All good dads wrestle their sons. When God gave Jacob a new name He also blessed him, but only after He wrestled with him (Genesis 32:22-32). With that new identity Jacob ("Israel") would build a great nation (Israel actually means "He who wrestles with God"). But to wrestle you must get close and strain as you trust your dad won't hurt you. He's making you. Who better to answer "who am I" than the author of all men who knew you before you were born? Trust the process as you lean into Him, just like a good dad... He let Jacob win, He wants you to win, too.

*The Trail in the Woods* is a gift to all sons, a culmination of learned lessons of the woods as a backdrop for God's Word, both in exaltations and warnings, to men. From Solomon's pursuit of wisdom to Paul's admonition against anxiety, His words are reflected in His creation, His woods. Read closely and you will note that there are actual survival techniques sprinkled within the lines. *The Trail* is a reminder of Christ's promise to be "*a lampstand to our feet*" (Psalm 119:105) and that only He is "*the Way*" (John 14:6). The poem is read in seven syllable (heptasyllabic) lines. Scriptural references serve as a key to follow the poem's roots.

**How To Seek:**

Before you begin reading, I want to challenge you to truly seek. One of the greatest promises ever recorded in scripture is *"seek ye first the kingdom of God and all these other things will be added to you."* (Mathew 6:33). Although this scripture references things (food, clothes, etc.) in the prior verse, let's face it "all these other things" is pretty broad...everything we need! So, if God's currency is faith, then perhaps one of the greatest spiritual transactions is...*seeking.* Here are some tips on how to seek:

SEEK

- **Three Times**: We see "three times" a lot in scripture. Whether it was Jonah in the belly of a whale for three days, the Holy Trinity (Father, Son and Holy Spirit) or that Jesus was resurrected on the third day, three is used a lot in the Bible. I encourage you to seek God three times in what is, admittedly, a pretty short read.

WISDOM

- **Meditate on His word**: All through scripture we are directed to *"meditate day and night on His word"* (Joshua 1:8). The Hebrew word here "Hagah" actually means to "chew the cud". It means if something has yet to digest, to continue to, (literally) CHEW ON IT. You are no doubt imagining a cow lying in a field, relaxed and...ruminating. Don't strain, just relax and...be the cow (sorry, just had to).

WRESTLE

- **An Intimate Father who Wants to be found**: We often think God is hiding from us. There was a time that I was mad at God not physically showing Himself to me. It wasn't till later that I learned that God actually tried that. "In Genesis 3:8-9 we see it may have been custom for God to walk daily in the garden. Even asking *"why are you hiding"* even after Adam and Eve had sinned. It is not He who hides but often us as we see our sin makes Him unapproachable without Christ. Now we must know Him by His Word, His spirit, His true identity, His presence. His physical features, alone, just weren't enough for us. *"I revealed myself to those who did not ask for me; I was found by those who did not seek me. To a nation that did not call on my name, I said, 'Here am I, here am I.'"* (Isaiah 65:1). He wants to be found, but our part is to seek.

FIND

- **Hear It:** I have been asked to make this book in audio form. I believe there is much to learn from listening "Whoever has ears let him hear" (Matthew 11:15) and *"faith comes by hearing."* (Romans 10:17). Whether you are trying to track the rhyme and meter or simply are on the road…listen in by accessing the audio version at <u>www.thetrailinthewoods.com</u>

Just like a stroll through the woods, be inquisitive and enjoy the walk with your Father. Although instructional in parts, just receive wisdom and know He sees you and loves you.

**How to Receive: "Write This Down".**

Knowing how to receive is vital. Whether it's receiving a compliment, a gift, or even correction, God puts a great deal of value on "RECEIVING". It's more important than food: *"Man shall not live on bread alone, but on every word that comes from the mouth of God."* (Matthew 4:4). There are things I seek now that my younger self simply wouldn't accept, much less write down. Although I have heard from friends how much closer their walk has been since they started journaling, I never did it. I enjoy writing, but never journaled because the very word "journaling" felt feminine to me.

A couple of years ago my sister-in-law gave me a journal. It was leather with parchment paper inside and looks…well, manly. So now, as things are revealed to me, I write them down. But I must confess, this is recent. It has been a blessing to walk things out with the Lord by writing down my thoughts as I receive what He has shared. I was missing a gift. Whether you want to write anywhere in this book, or write in the "Notes" section in the back, receive by writing.

*Then the LORD said to Moses, "Write this on a scroll as something to be remembered…" Exodus 17:14*

To the son who receives this, someone loves you fiercely and they want the best for you. There are things in this life you won't want to experience for yourself. Although you still will, this is a gift to help you to avoid unneeded scars (Proverbs 5:9–14). I've often been asked, "How do I start reading the Bible?" I've always wanted to answer, "would you like to go hunting?" My prayer is that this writing blesses those who read it.

*Look to the Lord and His strength; seek His face always.* (1 Chronicles 16:11)

Keep seeking.

# *Another Book?*

*I don't like to read books. It's a sad irony that I've written one. Yup, another hypocrite. Most great books I've read were a requirement, only to eventually engage them voraciously as I sensed their strength. Truth is, early on in a book, I am looking for a reason to put it down. So if you're like me, this page is for you.*

## WHAT IF I DON'T HAVE A "FATHER"

It could be the very word brings about pain. Whether it was an absentee father, a wound or a missed childhood—these are real hurts that often keep us from trusting anything with that name. You may even be fearful of becoming a father one day. The Jews called the Most High God, "Abba". This term is the equivalent of "daddy", a very intimate, very personal, very relational father. HE is the template of the best dad: *"slow to anger, abounding in love"* (Psalm 103:8). No father can match Him. Maybe you are just fearful of being duped: a father? I challenge you not to be duped into thinking you don't have one—the best. Step into the woods and see for yourself.

## I JUST DON'T LIKE POETRY—NOT MY GENERATION

This isn't just poetry, it's a riddle with survival techniques. The words point to "life cheats" much like shortcuts in a video game...of life. Read the words to figure the key. Add a beat and it's a rap! Truth is still truth—you're going to want to know this stuff.

## NOTE TO SPIRITUAL FATHERS

You are giving a gift. You no doubt had someone speak into your life, a coach, a pastor, a father of a friend, or someone who noticed you. Do not shirk or be intimidated—you are now that man.

*"Greater love has no one than this: to lay down one's life for one's friends"* (John 15:13). Could this also mean to carve out a piece of your life (time) for another's journey? I think it does. You may feel inadequate. Let me put those fears at bay…you are. We all are. He is our Father too, point to Him. Bless and be blessed.

## NOTE TO DADS
WHAT IF I HAVE BEEN AN ABSENTEE DAD? You are here now. Start now. Do not compare yourself with other dads. Comparison is a thief, the only results you will get are either pride or shame, neither spirit is of God. You have now…right now. Don't miss this.

WHAT IF I DON'T KNOW THE BIBLE? Great, take the journey too. This is a safe place to explore scripture. If something really compels you to read further—dive deeper. Funny thing, you will see wisdom that you've heard your whole life but in a different way. The Word is simply the origin of that wisdom—you'll recognize much of it.

WHAT IF I AM ALREADY THE BEST DAD EVER? Then provide a gift that your son can make his own as he walks his journey. You no doubt still feel like he's not ready. He's not. Neither were you. Equip him, be present and trust that God knows exactly what He is doing. Truth: He is more His than yours.

STILL NOT COMPELLED? Just a Step
*"Give this command to the priests who carry the Ark of the Covenant: 'When you reach the banks of the Jordan River, take a few steps into the river and stop there.'"* (Joshua 3:8). Everything God promised the Jews was just on the other side of the Jordan. But they had to step in. Trust that God only calls you to something on the other side of faith: it is better than where you find yourself standing…even now. Your only responsibility is the first step of faith. Step in.

## THE TRAIL GUIDE: How To Begin

I don't know where your faith is right now. You may be at the "God, if you're out there" point in your life OR "Jesus, I just want to see you in my life". Regardless, I challenge you to specifically call on the name of Jesus before you begin.

1. **Read the poem by subject** ("Embark", "Nourish", etc.) aloud, then look over the scripture in the margin that it references. You'll see the small numbers in the poem throughout the book. If you want more context to that scripture, reference a Bible or you can google it (there are many great Bible apps as well). I use the New International Version (NIV), but you may find other versions to be easier reading like the NKJV or the NASV. Anytime you see a reference to a *scripture, it will be in italics*. I challenge you to look it up for yourself to see how it speaks to you.
2. **Mark it up**: Make notes wherever you like- this book is yours. If you have an image that the poem or scripture gives you, draw it if you like. Give your book life, personalize it.
3. **The Trail Guide**: At the end of each subject you will see "The Trail Guide". There will be some commentary, maybe a story of how this wisdom worked in someone else's life, along with some questions. There may be a CHALLENGE or SURVIVAL TIP for application in your own journey.

*"But when he, the Spirit of truth, comes, he will guide you into all the truth. He will not speak on his own; he will speak only what he hears, and he will tell you what is yet to come." (John 16:13)*

# Enter the Trail: Doorways

As you seek, God will show you doorways in this life. What makes that even more powerful is that the doors God opens, no one can shut and the ones He shuts, no man can open (Revelation 3:7). Be careful walking past doors you know He has opened. They are powerful gifts. Be equally careful trying to open doors He has closed, there are seasons in life that must be moved through so that you may get to where He's called you. It takes faith to leave where you are, even a bad place. To grow means that you can't stay here. Time to grow…time to go.

Enter the trail.

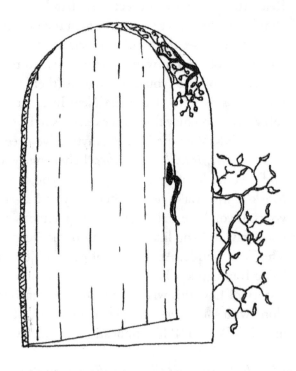

*"Ask, and it will be given to you; seek, and you will find; knock, and it will be opened to you. For everyone who asks receives, and he who seeks finds, and to him who knocks it will be opened."* Matthew 7:7-8

# The Trail in the Woods

A great sin of old men's ways,
Withheld fruit of learned days
And pass to grave what was taught,
So then the son oft' repays[1]

Thus hereby I set in print,
Marks and signs, Creator's hint[2]
That you may here glimpse the glint,
Glory light of Son was sent

Your trek will oft' seem to fail,
Snares and arrows will assail[3]
Time in the woods will prevail,
Spent therein upon the Trail.[4]

[1] The proverbs of Solomon son of David, king of Israel: for gaining wisdom and instruction; for understanding words of insight; for receiving instruction in prudent behavior, doing what is right and just and fair; for giving prudence to those who are simple, knowledge and discretion to the young—let the wise listen and add to their learning, and let the discerning get guidance—for understanding proverbs and parables, the sayings and riddles of the wise. The fear of the Lord is the beginning of knowledge, but fools despise wisdom and instruction. (Prov. 1:1–7)

[2] For since the creation of the world God's invisible qualities--his eternal power and divine nature--have been clearly seen, being understood from what has been made, so that people are without excuse. (Rom. 1:20)

[3] Opponents must be gently instructed, in the hope that God will grant them repentance leading them to a knowledge of the truth, and that they will come to their senses and escape from the trap of the devil, who has taken them captive to do his will. (2 Tim. 2:25–26)

[4] Thomas said to him, "Lord, we don't know where you are going, so how can we know the way?" Jesus answered, "I am the way and the truth and the life. No one comes to the Father except through me. (John 14:5–6)

# *Prepare*

Don the helmet, sword and shield;
Breastplate snug—prepare to wield
Spirit sword will cut to chaff,
Strongholds which refuse to yield[5]

Cloak thy shoulders with the zeal,[6]
Steady gait with even keel
Treasure built beyond the clouds,
Neither rust nor thief can steal[7]

Cold crisp morning's
bite will greet,
Sojourn step with unshod feet
Tether about shoes of peace,
Set out on the wooded peat.[8]

[5] Finally, be strong in the Lord and in his mighty power. Put on the full armor of God, so that you can take your stand against the devil's schemes. For our struggle is not against flesh and blood, but against the rulers, against the authorities, against the powers of this dark world and against the spiritual forces of evil in the heavenly realms. Therefore put on the full armor of God, so that when the day of evil comes, you may be able to stand your ground, and after you have done everything, to stand. Stand firm then, with the belt of truth buckled around your waist, with the breastplate of righteousness in place, and with your feet fitted with the readiness that comes from the gospel of peace. In addition to all this, take up the shield of faith, with which you can extinguish all the flaming arrows of the evil one. Take the helmet of salvation and the sword of the Spirit, which is the word of God. And pray in the Spirit on all occasions with all kinds of prayers and requests. With this in mind, be alert and always keep on praying for all the Lord's people. (Eph. 6:10–18)

[6] Never be lacking in zeal, but keep your spiritual fervor, serving the Lord. (Rom. 12:11)

[7] Do not store up for yourselves treasures on earth, where moths and vermin destroy, and where thieves break in and steal. But store up for yourselves treasures in heaven, where moths and vermin do not destroy, and where thieves do not break in and steal. (Matt. 6:19–20)

[8] I will give you every place where you set your foot, as I promised Moses. (Josh. 1:3)

## The Trail Guide: PREPARE:

Ever woke up and you just know it's going to be a good day? What about a bad day? Did you notice that you were often right based upon what you had already decided? In "Prepare" we see the need to actually "put on" the armor that God provides every day: Faith, Righteousness, the Sword of Truth, etc. Growing up playing high school football we were always reminded to check our gear before the game started. No one would ever dream of taking the field without their equipment. You could get hurt. Imagine that your mind is the field of combat (the scrimmage). God wants us to know that this life can be a spiritual war zone. No one belongs on the field without their gear nor in the woods without the right tools. In Christ, God provides us with this gear! Suit up every day first thing in the morning, set your mind right and expect great things. In this way we prepare our spirit to protect our mind.

When you get up in the morning, what are typically your first thoughts?

_____

_____

_____

_____

How could the *"Sword of Truth"* in Ephesians 6:7 (God's Word) cut through confusions regarding tough decisions? What are some of the decisions you are struggling with now?

_____

_____

_____

_____

Where's your treasure? The world often tells us we aren't enough because we don't have enough. This can often lure us into a lifetime of striving for the wrong thing. In Mathew 6: 19-20 we are reminded of treasures (eternal ones) that are more valuable. If your time and talent were money, where are you investing those now? How could you make deposits for more than just the temporary? How might that change how you start your day?

_____

_____

_____

_____

CHALLENGE: I challenge you to wake up in time to prepare your mind for the day. Pray about what you wrote above, about what's on your mind. If a thought interrupts your prayer, pray about that thought.

SURVIVAL TIP: Spend time sharpening your knife before using it. The most dangerous knife can be a dull one. Use a wet stone with a little spit, as you draw the blade away from you with circular or crescent shaped strokes as you hone the edge.

*Tools for the Trail: No pack should be without the following- knife, flint based firestick, kindling, twine, fishing hooks, compass, 1st aid, metal cook pot and an ax or bow saw.*

# Sharpening A Knife

An edge is not created, it is revealed as material is taken away. When we "sharpen" something we are actually taking away metal with friction. Just as in true relationship with other men of God, we often sharpen each other as *"iron sharpens iron, so one man sharpens another"* (Proverbs 27:17). This could mean friction, conflict in brotherly love, in order to reveal our best selves. It's often not what needs to be added, it's what needs to go- to be sharpened.

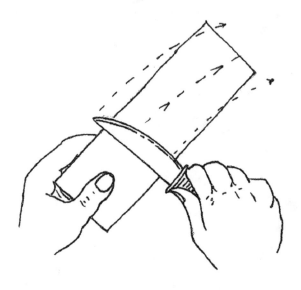

Using a sharpening stone or "wetstone", always have the tang side (the dull side) of the knife toward your hand bracing the stone. Whether you draw the blade forward or backward, you will see an edge forming at the front of the blade as you swipe in a semicircle direction to hone the blade from "heel" (the bottom) to the "point" (the top) of the edge. The higher the angle, the stronger the edge... the lower...the sharper.

# Embark

Mark well where you
start your quest,
Make haste but leave time for rest[9]
Not alone, as iron's need,[10]
Makes a man his very best

Mark thy heading is true East,
Spend not moments fearing beast
Walk in the Light,[11] seek the Trail,
They won't harm you in the least

Misplaced steps may
sometimes find,
Consequences none too kind
Renew your thoughts[12]
every morn,[13]
Your wounds and scars
He will bind.

[9] In peace I will lie down and sleep, for you alone, LORD, make me dwell in safety. (Psalm 4:8)

[10] As iron sharpens iron, so one person sharpens another. (Prov. 27:17)

[11] This is the message we have heard from him and declare to you: God is light; in him there is no darkness at all. If we claim to have fellowship with him and yet walk in the darkness, we lie and do not live out the truth. But if we walk in the light, as he is in the light, we have fellowship with one another, and the blood of Jesus, his Son, purifies us from all sin. If we claim to be without sin, we deceive ourselves and the truth is not in us. (1 John 1:5–8)

[12] Do not conform to the pattern of this world, but be transformed by the renewing of your mind. Then you will be able to test and approve what God's will is—his good, pleasing and perfect will. (Rom. 12:2)

[13] Because of the Lord's great love we are not consumed, for his compassions never fail. They are new every morning; great is your faithfulness. (Lam. 3:22–23)

## The Trail Guide: EMBARK

I love a good road trip, from packing the car to getting my snacks together and a good playlist. I call it "road mode". Do you have a sequence to starting your day? Maybe it's a work out or maybe its playing a game "snoozing" your alarm till you're late. Or maybe you start in God's word, even if just for a few minutes. In "EMBARK" we see the encouragement to "make haste but leave time for rest". ("REST" is a command we'll talk about later. Also, the best road trips aren't alone. You'll need someone to "sharpen" you. More of that in "ALLIES, FRIENDS and FOES"). In short, set your mind on the destination and don't do this life alone. Don't have anyone like that yet? As you chase eternal things, you will look up and see others on the same path...they're looking for you too.

Name a goal, that you could make at the beginning of every day, to keep your mind set on eternal things. Write it in "active speech". (Example: I begin every day with...)

_____

_____

_____

_____

*"Walking in the Light"* (1 John 1:7) often means not hiding anything. You can't kick Satan out of the dark, it's his backyard. What things could you bring into the light by sharing them in prayer or with a friend? It's ok to write a "code word" or two into the space below that only you and God know what it means.

_____

_____

_____

"Misplaced Steps": What if I screw up?: It's ok, because you're going to. It's a part of the journey. The hockey great Wayne Gretzky was once quoted, "You miss one hundred percent of the shots you don't take." The truth is that fear kills dreams. Your best life (the blessings, the people, the identity) are just on the other side of this chasm called "fear". You are going to make mistakes and God knows this. But the biggest is holing up on the sideline of life and missing out because you may mess up. When you do make mistakes, the Lord will heal you and use that error for something good (Romans 8:28). That is what grace is.

How would your life look if you decided fear was not going to be a part of it? How would this change how you started each day?

_____

_____

_____

SURVIVAL TIP: Prepare for mistakes by giving yourself grace to make them. Before you go into the woods, always let someone know when you plan to emerge. Whether a few hours or weeks. No one sends help for someone they don't know is missing.

# *Mind*

Canopied dark, smell the air;
Blanket o'grief men despair
Self-pitied sloth sit with death[14],
Do not stop or tarry there

Briars will grab from forest floor,
Barbs will search your every pore
Holding you to mourn your pain,
Draw they sword, create the door[15]

Duck through dens of
dreary thought,
Crown of life already bought[16]
Paid for by a crown of thorns,
Smile and think of
what is sought.[17]

[14] For by the grace given me I say to every one of you: Do not think of yourself more highly than you ought, but rather think of yourself with sober judgment, in accordance with the faith God has distributed to each of you. (Rom. 12:3)

[15] We are hard pressed on every side, but not crushed; perplexed, but not in despair; persecuted, but not abandoned; struck down, but not destroyed. (2 Cor. 4:8–9)

[16] Blessed is the one who perseveres under trial because, having stood the test, that person will receive the crown of life that the Lord has promised to those who love him. (James 1:12)

[17] But seek first his kingdom and his righteousness, and all these things will be given to you as well. (Matt. 6:33)

# The Trail Guide: MIND

Loss, death and grief are a part of this broken world, but we aren't built to stay in those places. I lost my late wife in September of 2016. One of the things God taught me in that season of life was that I was not built to remain eternally in grief. I had seen people who had lost their loved ones remain in a constant state of mourning. It became their identity. Grief often gave way to self-pity and then to emptiness. I knew I couldn't do that as I still had people counting on me, including my kids. So I asked God to show me what was keeping me in that state of mind. For me it was self-pity and sensing the pity of others. It made me angry that I would become "that poor guy" if I allowed self-pity to define me. I missed my wife, but I knew she was doing better than I (*"apart from the body, at home with the Lord"* 2 Cor. 5:8) and that she would want me to continue to run hard till my race was done, and it wasn't. I had to pivot. The Word ("the Sword") helped me. If you are mourning something that you think should have been, God knows how that feels. Allow Him to get close. *"The Lord comforts the brokenhearted and saves those who are crushed in spirit."* (Psalm 34:18 )

Do you have something or someone you are mourning? A dream? A life? A person? A wound? Please write about what that is below:

_____

_____

_____

_____

Like a backpack full of weight that was not meant for you to carry, how would offloading that to Jesus change the way you walked your life?

_____

_____

_____

_____

Read James 1:12: How might overcoming this hurt change the way you see yourself as a beloved son? How might life look without the weight of that hurt?

_____

_____

_____

_____

SURVIVAL TIP: Lay it down! Some things are just too heavy to carry all the time. When packing for a journey, minimize the weight you carry by prioritizing that which you can't live without. Excess weight increases your caloric burn, calories are what keep you going.

CHALLENGE: I challenge you to pray the following prayer as a way to start the transaction of allowing Jesus to bare this burden for you:

Jesus, I am hurt about the loss of _____. This sorrow is too big for me to carry and I can't think of a safe place to put it accept with you. Will you please take it from me? When I think of that burden, I ask that your Holy Spirit remind me that it's now yours. Thank you for walking alongside me in this Lord. I pray this in Jesus name. Amen.

# *Nourish*

Fuel thy body with the Bread,[18]
Drop to your knees,
bow your head
Time for prayer, refuel the mind,
Trusting steps as you are fed[19]

Shutes of green dine in their life,
Death's diet is worried strife
Feed upon the thoughts of joy,[20]
Fear and filth put to the knife[21]

Living water must be found,[22]
Seek you out the lower ground
Life within is safe to drink,
Taste not creeks which
make no sound.

[18] Very truly I tell you, the one who believes has eternal life. I am the bread of life. Your ancestors ate the manna in the wilderness, yet they died. But here is the bread that comes down from heaven, which anyone may eat and not die. I am the living bread that came down from heaven. Whoever eats this bread will live forever. This bread is my flesh, which I will give for the life of the world. (John 6:47–51)

[19] Trust in the Lord with all your heart and lean not on your own understanding; in all your ways submit to him, and he will make your paths straight. (Prov. 3:5–6)

[20] Finally, brothers and sisters, whatever is true, whatever is noble, whatever is right, whatever is pure, whatever is lovely, whatever is admirable—if anything is excellent or praiseworthy—think about such things. Whatever you have learned or received or heard from me, or seen in me—put it into practice. And the God of peace will be with you. (Phil. 4:8–10)

[21] We demolish arguments and every pretension that sets itself up against the knowledge of God, and we take captive every thought to make it obedient to Christ. (2 Cor. 10:5)

[22] On the last and greatest day of the festival, Jesus stood and said in a loud voice, "Let anyone who is thirsty come to me and drink. Whoever believes in me, as Scripture has said, rivers of living water will flow from within them." (John 7:37–38)

# The Trail Guide: NOURISH

To survive in the woods, you must be conscious of your fuel: both food and water. Their consumption, quality and the rate at which you spend them (the calories you burn) will determine your survival. The things we feed ourselves also relates to what we ingest mentally and spiritually. Wrong fuel: wrong outcome. In NOURISH we see the things that press us forward (prayer, joy) and the things that drain us and rob us like pornography ("filth") and worry (more on that in "EMPTINESS AND ANXIETY"). Answer the questions below and then fuel up on "Joy" in the CHALLENGE!

According to the American Psychological Association, chronic stress is linked to the six leading causes of death: heart disease, cancer, lung ailments, accidents, cirrhosis of the liver and suicide. Furthermore, more than 75 percent of all physician office visits are for stress-related ailments and complaints. So what does that mean to you and me? It means our mind is the battlefield by which the day is won and lost. What are you feeding it?

After reading the scriptural references for NOURISH, how can we have "trusting steps" in this life?

_____

_____

_____

_____

In Philippians 4:8-10, we see a list of things to think on. How would thinking on these things affect your journey? How would it affect how you interact with people and challenges?

_____

_____

_____

_____

SURVIVAL TIP: You must have water! At least 60% of the adult body is made of water and it's a requirement to keep functioning. But stagnant water is an incubator for bacteria including mosquito larvae and other nasty critters. It's best to charcoal filter or boil water before drinking. If you can't do this, at least make sure the water is moving like a stream. A spring fed stream is the best. (Jesus talks about *"living water"* in John 7:37-39.)

CHALLENGE: Paul wrote a book (a letter) in the Bible called "Philippians". It is so upbeat and encouraging that it has been called "the joy epistle". The irony is that Paul wrote about "Joy" while he was in jail! I challenge you to simply read the first four chapters of Philippians. I promise it will fill your cup. (Ok, the truth is there's only four chapters).

# *Rest*

Eyes to the Son e'en at night,
You may still then see the Light[23]
Reflection of fairer moon,
Glows through darkness
giving sight

Through darkest trek
source the flame,[24]
Tinder sparked and fuel to claim
Boughs of leaves repel the drops,
Warm your bones with Jesus name

Rest is not just counting sand,
Not suggestion but command[25]
Place your burdens at the cross,
Only there faith's flame is fanned

Cleft of rock set to your back,
Spread the scent to thwart attack
Warming stones for bed at night,
Accept Peace or sleep you'll lack[26].

[23] This is the message we have heard from him and declare to you: God is light; in him there is no darkness at all. (1 John 1:5)

[24] They asked each other, "Were not our hearts burning within us while he talked with us on the road and opened the Scriptures to us?" (Luke 24:32)

[25] Come to me, all you who are weary and burdened, and I will give you rest. (Matt. 11:28)

[26] Do not be anxious about anything, but in every situation, by prayer and petition, with thanksgiving, present your requests to God. And the peace of God, which transcends all understanding, will guard your hearts and your minds in Christ Jesus. (Phil. 4:6–7)

## The Trail Guide: REST

Did you know that rest is a commandment? When God built heaven and earth in six days, the word says *"on the seventh day He rested from all His work"* (Genesis 2:2). Why would the Creator need to rest? I don't think He needed to. Like a good Father He was modeling for us how He wanted us to live. The Hebrew word for rest is *"Shabat"* which actually interprets in English to "STOP". The world we live in is busy and always moving, always advertising always buzzing. Our electronic devices beckon our every waking hour. I know in my life, this "busyness" can become an idol as I make it my identity. God tells us to *"be still"* (Psalm 46:10, Exodus 14:14) because He loves us and has more for us than busyness and running hard. We often don't know what we are missing till we enter into His rest.

Why do you think God would command us to rest, to *"be still"*?

_____

_____

_____

_____

Are there battles in your life that seem like no matter what you do, they just persist? What would laying those at the foot of the cross look like for you?

_____

_____

_____

_____

Read Philippians 4:6-8. When we are thankful in prayer, we acknowledge God's strength. How might this protect our hearts and minds with the *"peace of God that transcends understanding"*?

_____

_____

_____

_____

SURVIVAL TIP: The poem talks about traveling at night if the moon is bright. Not only might this help you to avoid the sun's heat, it could preserve water and calories. But sometimes you just have to sleep. While you still have light find a good place to bed down and gather fuel for a fire starting with good kindling up to larger dry branches. Marking the area with your scent can help keep unwanted animals from visiting your camp. In cold conditions, place some larger stones close (but not too close) to the fire that you can kick over to your bedding for warmth through the night before you go to sleep. Pray for a good night sleep, then accept His peace.

# Making a Fire

A good flint rod or "steel striker" can be invaluable in the woods. First gather your tinder which can be small pieces of dry paper, tree bark or dried leaves. Ball this up as your "tinder nest". It's good to already have dry "kindling" (small twigs and brush), as well as your dry branches and logs so you can be ready to give your fire life. Once your tinder nest catches a flame, follow the chart below. Make sure the fire get's air- just not too much.

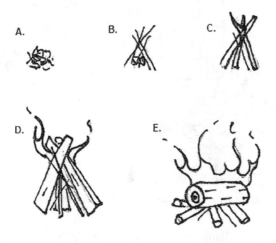

A. TINDER "NEST"- DRIED LEAVES, ETC.    B. TEE PEE TWIGS AND OTHER KINDLING

C. TEE PEE LARGER TWIGS/BRANCHES    D. TEE PEE LOGS WITH ONE LARGER LOG

E. LARGER LOG BECOMES "HEART" OF YOUR FIRE

# Shelter: Lean-To with Firewall

Check the prevailing wind to determine the opening of your lean-to to avoid excessive smoke from the fire you will build.

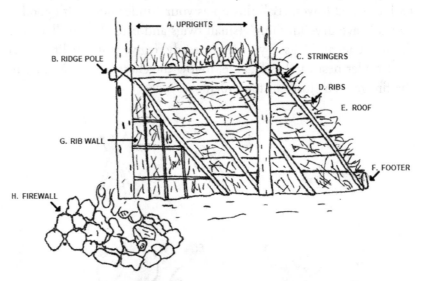

A. Uprights: Two sturdy trees, no less than 3" in diameter are the base. Their distance from one another to be a bit longer than your length laying down.

B. Ridge Pole: 3" diameter or larger should stick out 6" on each side of your uprights. Lash the ridgepole horizontally to the uprights about a foot higher than your waist.

C. Stringers: Stringers go from the ridge pole to the ground and create the depth and angle of your lean-to.

D. Ribs: Weave these flexible branches and vines horizontally to strengthen the shelter.

E. Roof: From the bottom to the top place evergreen boughs and leafy branches to create a rain shed. Repeat till sturdy and covered.

F. Footer: A heavier log placed at the foot of the shed to pin the bottom of your lean-to.

G. Rib Wall: Vertical stakes and brush to create a wind break and conserve heat.

H. Firewall: Stacked stones direct the heat of a fire toward the lean-to.

# *Hunt*

As morn breaks, you'll
see faint sign,
Bent grass and tracks mud malign
Soft edge speaks the track is fresh,
Heart rates rise and
thoughts incline

"Rise, kill, eat"[27] His
stores provide,
Soft step foot with every stride
To track the prey, see its thoughts,
Find the place where
game will hide

Kill not that which won't be used,
Poor stewardship unexcused[28]
His creatures are in your care,
Or empty bag, meal refused.

[27] Then a voice told him, "Get up, Peter. Kill and eat." (Acts 10:13)

[28] Then God said, "Let us make mankind in our image, in our likeness, so that they may rule over the fish in the sea and the birds in the sky, over the livestock and all the wild animals, and over all the creatures that move along the ground." So God created mankind in his own image, in the image of God he created them; male and female he created them. God blessed them and said to them, "Be fruitful and increase in number; fill the earth and subdue it. Rule over the fish in the sea and the birds in the sky and over every living creature that moves on the ground." (Gen. 1:26–28)

# The Trail Guide: HUNT

I remember the first time I took the life of an animal for food. I was both exhilarated and saddened. The truth is that when God told Adam to *"subdue the earth"* (Genesis 1:28) it was meant as both a blessing and a role of responsibility. So, when you sense the awe of God's creation, including His animals…our game; it is a beautiful thing of reverence for that provision. Ironically, many of these hunting tips are the same way to hunt truth. In dark times, truth can be equally hidden and may be more important than any meal you could miss. Hunt both game and truth by *"giving thought to your steps"* (Proverbs 14:15).

TIP: **You are the loudest and scariest thing in creation**. *"I praise you because I am fearfully and wonderfully made, your works are wonderful, I know that full well."* (Psalm 139:14). This means the quieter you are (in sound, scent and sight) the more likely you may get to eat. A squirrel may hear you first, but he will likely first see your face and hands as their glare doesn't fit in the woods. A little mud and you are camouflaged. The less you disturb creation, the better hunter and steward you become.

Why is it important to eat what we kill and not just take life for sport? Should we hunt predators like coyotes and bobcats if they threaten our livestock? Why or why not?

---

---

---

TIP: **See the story in the woods**. The woods can tell you a story about the life that has traveled there. Whether its where deer bedded down the night before (larger areas of matted down grass), tracks or even rooted up areas (hogs know best where grubs are located) the earth will write a story if you look closer. Small holes at the base of tall grass are often trails for smaller game like rabbits or squirrels which can be a great place to set a snare.

QUESTION: What are you Hunting? If our lives and decisions are chasing after the things of this world: *"lust of the flesh, lust of the eyes and pride of life"* (I John 2:16), we will eventually come face to face with what we were tracking. What would your time and passion say you are hunting after daily?

_____

_____

_____

_____

It's always better to know what you are chasing after! Here are some tracks that you may find in the woods:

# Common Tracks

Below you will see some common tracks from the woods. One of the main differences from the canine family (dogs, wolves, coyotes and foxes) and felines (bobcats and mountain lions) is that the canines cannot retract their claws. No claws? It is a cat of some kind.

(NOT TO SCALE: NOTICE THE SHAPE DIFFERENCES)

Everything leaves behind a story, as we track it, we learn its behavior. Note the space between tracks. Deep, sloppy tracks spaced further apart? Your prey may know you are onto them.

# *Provision*

The pouch of coin trusted to,
As a tool, do not miscue
Parting faster than returns,
Squander not was given you[29]

The value there can be burned,
Only known is he that earned
Once it's gone the lesson learned,
Cost the price of that discerned

Do not see the gifts as owned,
Steward's blade of edge is honed
By seeing not these things thine,
For this life they are but loaned.[30]

[29] The wise store up choice food and olive oil, but fools gulp theirs down. (Prov. 21:20)

[30] Command those who are rich in this present world not to be arrogant nor to put their hope in wealth, which is so uncertain, but to put their hope in God, who richly provides us with everything for our enjoyment. (1 Tim. 6:17)

# The Trail Guide: PROVISION

"I hate money." I remember saying the words as I learned my mom and dad would be divorcing. I just knew it was because of money. We had lived both with and without money, but when the oil crash of 1986 hit, we lost our house, our cars and a lot of identity (false identity). I found myself sleeping on my grandparents' floor, along with my siblings, and I eventually saw my parents' relationship unravel. I spoke an oath (these can have ramifications) that I would earn enough money that my family would never fall apart. I later learned that it was not an absence of money that destroyed our family, it was the absence of the Lord as our guide through it. Growing up not knowing how to manage money, I made many mistakes I want you to avoid. I've also learned that too much money can be a challenge as we will have to give an answer for how we use it, and other resources, like time, talents and even discernment of scripture (Luke 12:48). Ultimately, God knows that *"where your treasure is, there will your heart be also"* (Luke 12:34). We must manage our resources well, while at no time making them our god. Never exchange that which is eternal for that which is temporary. In fact, anytime you can exchange temporary things for eternal ones, it's typically the best deal as we *"lay up our treasures in heaven"* (Matthew 6:19-21). Can't I enjoy my money? Sure you can, just don't make it your god...or your tormentor.

Notice Solomon's prayer below. Even with all his wealth, he wanted to be balanced in in his finances and honest in his dealings. *__8__Keep deception and lies far from me, Give me neither poverty nor riches Feed me with the food that is my portion, __9__That I not be full and deny You and say, "Who is the LORD?" Or that I not be in want and steal, And profane the name of my God.* (Proverbs 30:8-9)

CHALLENGE: Read the Parable of the Talents (Mathew 25: 14-30). Why do you think God gave differing amounts of talents to each servant?

_____

_____

_____

_____

The less I saw resources as mine, the easier it was to manage them. What is your greatest fear when trusting the Lord with your money and your needs? What is the risk of NOT trusting Him with them?

_____

_____

_____

_____

Make God your "Senior Partner" in all things "money". Faith is God's currency. It's how we show Him honor and, along with worship, the only thing we can really give Him that He doesn't already own. When God traded in faith with His people, they were to set aside 10% (a "tithe") for His church. God actually challenges us to *test me in this* (Malachi 3:10). I've never been able to out give God, you won't either.

SURVIVAL TIP: HUSTLE WINS AND EARNS: Money is just an exchange of value. All you have to do for it is serve someone else (ironically something we're already called to do) through a product or service. When you serve with your very best, you will develop a "brand". To get paid: 1. Show up ten minutes early 2. Do more than you are paid for 3. Ask for more work. You will always have a job.

# *Work*

Work for God not as for men,[31]
Provision finds way within
Your stewardship, pacts to acts,
Returns then time and again

You're valued not by
what you own,[32]
A seed's true worth is
when it's sewn[33]
Under soil, remains unseen,
Springing forth till then unknown.

[31] Whatever you do, work at it with all your heart, as working for the Lord, not for human masters. (Col. 3:23)

[32] Then he said to them, "Watch out! Be on your guard against all kinds of greed; life does not consist in an abundance of possessions." (Luke 12:15)

[33] So will it be with the resurrection of the dead. The body that is sown is perishable, it is raised imperishable; it is sown in dishonor, it is raised in glory; it is sown in weakness, it is raised in power. (1 Cor. 15:42–43)

# The Trail Guide: WORK

I remember watching my dad work the land at our house in East Texas. I was bewildered with his passion to be in the heat from hand clearing brush to driving a tractor, for hours. Why would anyone want to work that hard? Later that summer I ended up hauling hay with my dad and some of my buddies. It was the hardest work I ever did. But, for the first time in my young life, I felt like I had a say in how my life may work out. I remember the cash being counted out to each worker. It was the first day that I ever felt like a real man.

*"For even when we were with you, we gave you this rule: The one who is unwilling to work shall not eat."* (2 Thessalonians 3:10). Why do you think God puts value on working?

_____

_____

_____

*"Whatever you do, work at it with all your heart, as working for the Lord, not for human masters"* (Colossians 3:23). How can our work ethic reflect on our faith?

_____

_____

_____

In Proverbs Solomon tells us that work is a blessing from God (Ecclesiastes 2:24). How has work blessed you? Take a minute to pray and ask God where you can serve. How has he equipped you to help someone else whether it's a person, a ministry or charity?

_____

_____

_____

_____

SURVIVAL TIP: Build Your Brand: Some of the most well-known names in business today can spend on average of over $4 Billion dollars annually to build and maintain their "brand". Why would they do that? You may not know it, but you were born with a "business" of your own. How you treat others, how you serve and keep commitments will build a brand and a "customer experience" to those around you. If you work for an employer, you still own your own business. They may just be your biggest customer. Build your brand daily.

CHALLENGE: Write down three ways you want your "Brand" (your work) to be known for:

1. _____

2. _____

3. _____

Bonus Tip: DWYSYWD: Do What You Say You Will Do…you'll beat 90% of the competition.

# *Allies, Friends and Foes*

Choose your ally, friend, and foe;[34]
Relationship rivers flow
Carries forth with time and trials,
Whom of them shall
heaven know?

Friends tack the compass heading,
Select saved for site's setting
Tho blessed to harbor hurt hearts,
Sin stifles moral heading[35]

A time for peace, a
time for flight,[36]
Times will come when
you must fight
The spirit foe, war to know,
Holy Spirit given sight.[37]

[34] Walk with the wise and become wise, for a companion of fools suffers harm. (Prov. 13:20)

[35] Do not be misled: "Bad company corrupts good character." (1 Cor. 15:33)

[36] A time to love and a time to hate, a time for war and a time for peace. (Eccles. 3:8)

[37] For our struggle is not against flesh and blood, but against the rulers, against the authorities, against the powers of this dark world and against the spiritual forces of evil in the heavenly realms. (Eph. 6:12)

## The Trail Guide: ALLIES, FRIENDS AND FOES

In the movie *"Lonesome Dove"*, there's a particular scene where Jake Spoon, a member of these once-great lawmen, leaves the group and falls in with a really bad gang. In a bizarre twist, the outlaws are caught by his old friends and Jake is about to share in the fate of these criminals when he pleads to his old captain, Augustus McRae. The captain replies, "You know how it works Jake, you ride with an outlaw, you die with an outlaw. I'm sorry you crossed the line." Jake's response is heart wrenching, "I didn't see no line, Gus." There is a difference between trying to help someone and "riding" with them. If you are repeatedly receiving bad counsel with bad examples, you will fall, and God knows this. The more we steep ourselves in darkness, it affects our ability to see the "lines" that can be crossed. Choose your friends as if you are choosing your best self. Can't find any? Become what you are looking for and you will find each other.

Do you think the friends you currently have will make you a better man? Why or why not?

_____

_____

_____

_____

In the scripture, *"Bad Company corrupts good morals"* (1 Corinthians 15:33), do you think Paul's warning is judgmental? Why or why not?

_____

_____

_____

_____

Read Proverbs 27:6 and 27:17. How could the *"wounds of a friend"* be faithful? How would "iron sharpen iron" when it comes to a real friend?

_____

_____

_____

_____

A FOE: You have an enemy. He has plans for you, but he only operates in darkness and deception. The name "Satan" actually means "accuser". He accuses us before the father *"day and night"* (Revelation 12:10) and speaks lies to us and others. Although you may see this behavior in others, remember that this is a spiritual war that we are in, not just *"flesh and blood"* (Ephesians 6:12). Battle against the enemy through the armor given you, see the enemy and speak against him and he will leave you (James 4:7). Know what you will stand for, know what you will not stand for and why. Be like-minded (Philippians 2:2)

CHALLENGE: Read Matthew 6:14-15. Pray for someone who has hurt you. This may seem hard. But do it in Christ's strength so that you may see how the real enemy deceived them into causing you pain. Forgive them. This will thwart the enemies plans in your life.

# A Mate

'Tis not good to be alone,[38]
Fruit won't fall from
hearts of stone
But do not lay in harlot's arms,
To her death you will be prone

Do not take an unyoked bride,[39]
Wandering spirits know no side
Taking flight at faintest fear,
Wielded wounds won't be denied

Cling to the doe[40] of youth's days,
To her fix your loving gaze
Lifting her within His strength,
Your walk of joy in His ways

Covenant eyes[41] to path stick,
Wayward women cut to quick
Only take your godly bride,
'Er' at heaven you will kick.[42]

[38] The Lord God said, "It is not good for the man to be alone. I will make a helper suitable for him." (Gen. 2:18)

[39] Do not be yoked together with unbelievers. For what do righteousness and wickedness have in common? Or what fellowship can light have with darkness? (2 Cor. 6:14)

[40] May your fountain be blessed, and may you rejoice in the wife of your youth. (Prov. 5:18)

[41] I made a covenant with my eyes, not to look lustfully at a young woman. (Job 31:1)

[42] …My husband is not at home; he has gone on a long journey. He took his purse filled with money and will not be home till full moon." With persuasive words she led him astray; she seduced him with her smooth talk. All at once he followed him like an ox going to the slaughter, like a deer stepping into a noose till an arrow pierces his liver, like a bird darting into a snare, little knowing it will cost him his life. Hamlet (Act 3 Scene 3) (Prov. 7:19–23)

## The Trail Guide: A MATE

In the last subject, we discussed choosing your friends wisely. However, the most important friend you will have in this life will be your wife. In Genesis, after God created all creatures and man, He said, *"It is not good for the man to be alone. I will make a helper suitable for him."* (Genesis 2:18). Before we assume that a helper is someone who just performs chores for us, let us understand that word more fully. The word, "helper" used in Aramaic (an ancient Hebrew language) is a variation of the same word that is used for the Holy Spirit: "Ezer Kenegdo". In other translations: "a warrior opposite, but complementary". Furthermore, once you take a wife you both will become *"one flesh"* (Genesis 2:24). Paul calls this a *"profound mystery"* (Ephesians 5:31-32) So, this decision, other than our decision to follow Christ, is the most important one of our lives. God made women beautiful. But if our only guide is chemistry (physical attraction) vs. calling (who does she follow), you could set yourself up to be wounded. Choose a wife who follows Christ.

In 2 Corinthians 6:14, Paul writes, *"Do not be yoked together with unbelievers"*. A yoke is an old-fashioned implement that was used to join together two oxen so that they could more easily do the work, together. How does this image change your perspective of taking a wife?

_____

_____

_____

_____

In the line "Wayward women cut to quick", how could having a physical relationship with someone who has no moral compass affect your life?

_____

_____

_____

_____

When Adam met Eve for the first time, he exclaimed "WO MAN!" That's how she got her name. Bad joke…sorry. But he did in fact say, "*This is now bone of my bones and flesh of my flesh; she shall be called 'woman,' for she was taken out of man.*" (Genesis 2:23). However, after Adam and Eve sinned ("the fall") he renamed her "Eve". This was not a compliment. After sin, Adam lost his bearing on who his wife REALLY was. She was him. His perfectly opposite, complementary…him. When we forget our wives are of us, not just for us, we lose our eyes for who they really are. They are beautifully and irreplaceably…us. Choose a wife wisely. If you already have, speak love over her. She is, after all, you too.

CHALLENGE: If you are single, list the things that are important to you in a wife.

_____

_____

_____

_____

If you are already married, cover your wife in prayer. Pray and speak identity over her. Other than just her physical beauty, list three names you see in her that are of God (if you aren't married, pray these names over your future wife):

1. _____

2. _____

3. _____

# *Avoid*

Greed can weaken warrior's will,
Sun will set to whippoorwill
Take eternal stock instead,[43]
Earth's trinkets can not fill

Wear not ye a champion's leaf,
Do not cause the Spirit grief[44]
Recall where from blessings came,
Never be a glory thief.

[43] But store up for yourselves treasures in heaven, where moths and vermin do not destroy, and where thieves do not break in and steal. (Matt. 6:20)

[44] Do not let any unwholesome talk come out of your mouths, but only what is helpful for building others up according to their needs, that it may benefit those who listen. And do not grieve the Holy Spirit of God, with whom you were sealed for the day of redemption. Get rid of all bitterness, rage and anger, brawling and slander, along with every form of malice. (Eph. 4:29–31)

# The Trail Guide: AVOID

There are traps in this life. The best trap is one that offers something easy...bait. We have an enemy and this enemy can't really create anything. There is only one Creator. So, what the enemy must do is twist, or spoil something that was given to us already. Although God created sex as a gift for a husband to intimately know his wife, Satan will try to use lust, pornography, and adultery to destroy or cheapen that bond. He will also try to use the blessing of abundance to create identity, to deceive us into thinking we are no one unless we have things and stuff. One of the places he has worked hard to make me stumble is: Greed. God placed a natural desire in our heart to build, to grow and prosper. However, when we replace God with these things, they become idols. It's ok to own some nice things, but they shouldn't own us. The lines in this poem are a reminder that wherever God is wanting to bless us, the enemy wants to rob us.

What are some things that you would like to accomplish in your lifetime?

---------------------------------------

---------------------------------------

---------------------------------------

---------------------------------------

Read over the list you wrote. How could these glorify God and keep you from being "robbed" by the enemy? How can you ensure those goals do not become idols?

_____

_____

_____

Glory Thief: In Acts 12:20-23, King Herod heard the applause of men as they gave him the glory that belonged to God. Herod did not correct the men, and he met with a horrible death. Why? "*God opposes the proud but shows favor to the humble*" (James 4:6). How can you sincerely give glory to God as you receive praise? Where could this be hard to do? Why?

_____

_____

_____

SURVIVAL TIP: Try this next time you receive praise for something God has done. First, say "thank you", then try saying "anything you see good in me is just Jesus using me anyway."

What is a snare that you know the enemy has tried to use on you?

_____

_____

_____

# Recognizing Poison

God provides ways to recognize things that are dangerous. Most things that are poisonous have an initial bitter or caustic taste. The reflex is to spit it out. If ingested sometimes the stomach may actually convulse to vomit it out- protecting us.

In other instances, whether it be poisonous snakes or vegetation-there is a way to identify the poisonous from the harmless. The following are rules that can be used:

Poison Ivy and Oak? "Leaves of three, let it be!"

Coral snakes (poisonous): "Red touch yellow, kill a fellow". King snake (non-poisonous) "red touch black, venom lack".

Here are a few ways to compare whether a snake is poisonous or non-venomous:

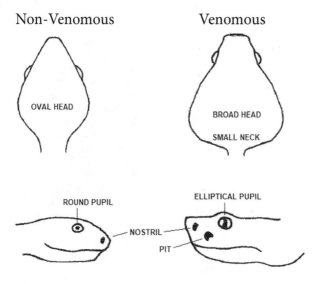

HINT: If you ever have to cut the head off of a snake, do not touch the head even after it is dispatched. That mouth can still instinctively bite you!

# The Tongue

Watch words that leave your lips,
Er' life or death from them slips[45]
Build a brother[46] with a bond,
To the Light his scales will tip

Rudder turns mighty vessel,[47]
Terms build truth's trestle
Sincere wounds of a friend,[48]
His sons God will wrestle.[49]

[45] The tongue has the power of life and death, and those who love it will eat its fruit. (Prov. 18:21)

[46] But encourage one another daily, as long as it is called "Today," so that none of you may be hardened by sin's deceitfulness. (Heb. 3:13)

[47] Or take ships as an example. Although they are so large and are driven by strong winds, they are steered by a very small rudder wherever the pilot wants to go. (James 3:4)

[48] Wounds from a friend can be trusted, but an enemy multiplies kisses. (Prov. 27:6)

[49] So Jacob was left alone, and a man wrestled with him till daybreak. When the man saw that he could not overpower him, he touched the socket of Jacob's hip so that his hip was wrenched as he wrestled with the man. Then the man said, "Let me go, for it is daybreak." But Jacob replied, "I will not let you go unless you bless me." The man asked him, "What is your name?" "Jacob," he answered. Then the man said, "Your name will no longer be Jacob, but Israel, because you have struggled with God and with humans and have overcome." Jacob said, "Please tell me your name." But he replied, "Why do you ask my name?" Then he blessed him there. (Gen. 32:24–29)

## The Trail Guide: THE TONGUE

And then I said it. "I hate you". It came right out of my mouth…to my mom…the one who carried me for nine months, fed me, bathed me, loved me no matter what. I know I said it because I was angry (she wouldn't let me ditch my responsibilities to go out with some friends). I wanted to hurt her…and I did. The bible talks about the tongue being one of the most powerful things we own. We can actually *"speak life"* or *"death"* over someone (Proverbs 18:21). In Matthew 5:22, God warns His children about this. Every person bears the image of God. We may disagree, we may see the enemy at work in another's life, but we have no authority to use our tongue as a weapon against another person as a curse.

*"The words of the reckless pierce like swords. But the tongue of the wise brings healing"* (Proverbs 12:18). How will you choose to use what you say to change lives?

_____

_____

_____

_____

Read Proverbs 18:21. The image in this scripture is of our having to actually "eat" our words. How is this so?

_____

_____

_____

_____

Read James 3:3-11. How is our tongue like the rudder of a ship? How is your tongue steering your life? How could you change it?

_____

_____

_____

_____

_____

Name a time when someone spoke something over you that changed how you saw yourself? Was it good or bad and how did it affect you?

_____

_____

_____

_____

_____

CHALLENGE: Accept what God says about you by reading aloud the following:

In Christ I was saved and called with a holy calling, not according to my works, "*but according to his own purpose and grace, which was given to me in Christ Jesus before time began.*" (2 Timothy 1:9)

Before he made the world, God loved me and chose me in Christ to be "*holy and without fault in his eyes.*" (Ephesians 1:4)

In Christ I am "*more than a conqueror through Him who loves me.*" (Romans 8:37)

In Christ I am "*a light of the world. A city set on a hill cannot be hidden.*" (Matthew 5:14)

In Christ I am a "*new creation. The old has passed away; behold, the new has come.*" (2 Corinthians 5:17)

In Christ I am God's "*workmanship, created in Christ Jesus for good works, which God prepared beforehand, that we should walk in them.*" (Ephesians 2:10)

In Christ I am "*one spirit with Him.*" (1 Corinthians 6:17)

In Christ I am a "*son of God, through faith.*" (Galatians 3:26)

# *Fear of Death*

Fearing frame's failing form,
Eternal heart is the norm[50]
Firm in faith alone will stand,[51]
Holding fast will stall the storm

Recall earth 'tis not your home,
His creation acres roam[52]
Death's shadow just
walk through,[53]
Triumph's text will fill your tome[54]

Death's a foe we all will face,
Earthly vessels will not grace
Heaven's door, we'll
need new flesh,
He provides[55] just run your race.[56]

[50] He has made everything beautiful in its time. He has also set eternity in the human heart; yet no one can fathom what God has done from beginning to end. (Eccles. 3:11)

[51] Be on your guard; stand firm in the faith; be courageous; be strong. (1 Cor. 16:13)

[52] The earth is the Lord's, and everything in it, the world, and all who live in it. (Ps. 24:1)

[53] Even though I walk through the darkest valley, I will fear no evil, for you are with me; your rod and your staff, they comfort me. (Ps. 23:4)

[54] Consider it pure joy, my brothers and sisters, whenever you face trials of many kinds, because you know that the testing of your faith produces perseverance. Let perseverance finish its work so that you may be mature and complete, not lacking anything. (James 1:2–4)

[55] For we know that if the earthly tent we live in is destroyed, we have a building from God, an eternal house in heaven, not built by human hands. Meanwhile we groan, longing to be clothed instead with our heavenly dwelling, because when we are clothed, we will not be found naked. For while we are in this tent, we groan and are burdened, because we do not wish to be unclothed but to be clothed instead with our heavenly dwelling, so that what is mortal may be swallowed up by life. Now the one who has fashioned us for this very purpose is God, who has given us the Spirit as a deposit, guaranteeing what is to come. (2 Cor. 5:1–5)

[56] I have fought the good fight, I have finished the race, I have kept the faith. (2 Tim. 4:7)

## The Trail Guide: FEAR OF DEATH

In the movie, *Braveheart*, William Wallace (played by Mel Gibson) is about to be executed. Queen Isabella begs him to reconsider his convictions to possibly save his life as she pleads, "but you will die". Wallace responds, "Every man dies. Not every man really lives". Although that is a really cool line, I know I don't want to die. I will also guess that you don't want to either. God has "*set eternity in the hearts of men*" (Ecclesiastes 3:11). The reason death is such a troubling subject is that we were built for eternity and anything short of that perplexes us, all of us. So, what do we do with this inevitable outcome we all must face? The truth is our souls will live forever, the real question is "where?" God stands outside of time; it does not affect Him. When man sinned, the bodies we occupy became temporary, they have a clock (Psalm 90:10). But, if we get so caught up in the end of our bodies' timeline, we will miss our eternal purpose (Ephesians 2:10). Once we trade that fear in, we can truly appreciate every day and moment as one with purpose and beauty.

Read 2 Timothy 1:7. Did you know that "fear" isn't just an emotion? It's a spirit! Fear's job is to thwart our purpose in Christ and twist our ability to think clearly. How could the fear of death keep you from your purpose?

_____

_____

_____

_____

*"For whoever wants to save their life will lose it, but whoever loses their life for me will save it."* (Matthew 16:25). In the context of what we've discussed, what do you think Jesus means by this?

_____

_____

_____

_____

In 2 Corinthians 5:1-10, Paul writes about our bodies being like a tent. That they wear out and how our soul longs for the *"imperishable"* new body God will give us. In 1 Corinthians 15: 42-44 Paul describes this new body. Why would God provide us with a new body?

_____

_____

_____

_____

SURVIVAL TIP: GETTING BIG means making yourself appear harder to attack. Predators seek easy prey. If you run from a cougar, wolf, bear or other deadly predator- they will likely give chase. Stand tall, spread your arms, talk loudly, make noise and slowly walk away. In the wild, fear can be a dinner bell for predators.

CHALLENGE: BIG GOD, BIG FAITH means we speak against fear. Repeat the following: "Spirit of Fear, you have no control over me. I will live out my purpose in joy. Leave me now, in the name of Jesus!"

# Emptiness and Anxiety

Anxious thoughts will
sometimes climb,
When to self you do resign
Praise and thanks[57] will
douse the dread
O'fires that fuel fear's design

Emptiness, the vacant sense,
Self-absorbed in present tense
From the Lord receive your call,[58]
Purpose found forever hence.

[57] Do not be anxious about anything, but in every situation, by prayer and petition, with thanksgiving, present your requests to God. And the peace of God, which transcends all understanding, will guard your hearts and your minds in Christ Jesus. (Phil. 4:6–7)

[58] Cast your cares on the Lord and he will sustain you; He will never let the righteous be shaken. (Ps. 55:22)

# The Trail Guide: EMPTINESS AND ANXIETY

Solomon, the wisest and wealthiest man to ever live, writes in Proverbs as he reflects on the emptiness of all his accomplishments: material wealth, women, accolades, fame… it's all a *"chasing after the wind"* (Ecclesiastes 1:14). Emptiness is the achievement of every carnal and material desire only to realize, "is that it?". It is the harsh conclusion of meaninglessness. Anxiety, on the other hand, is an orphan spirit that does not believe that we will be safe, cared for, seen—loved. Both are the inevitable realization that all this world has to offer is simply not enough. Ironically, these spiritual battles can be triggered by the perceived loss of identity or even the accomplishment of a life-long goal. One may ask, "Who am I, now?" The truth is that true fulfillment of our best self, purpose and identity only comes from our Designer, our Author, our Father. Christ describes this sweet spot in life as *"abundance"* (John 10:10), more than we need for more than we are. Both Emptiness and Anxiety are the result of thinking about one thing too much…ourselves. Being that God did not design us for only thinking of ourselves, it makes total sense that these are emotional dead ends. Ever met someone who seems to have everything, and yet they are miserable? The good news is that the opposite is also accurate. If we are true to our design and purpose, emptiness and anxiety lose their fuel. We were not created to be anxious, fearful or empty as they are tools of the enemy to distract us from our real purpose.

Where your eyes go, your body will follow: NASCAR drivers know this warning: "Never look at the wall". Our bodies and minds were built to go where our eyes take them. In defensive driving we are taught that, if we ever leave the road in an uncontrolled spin, to look for open spaces. In short, set your eyes on what you want- not what

you want to avoid. When we keep our eyes on God, we avoid emptiness and anxiety. When you worry, what are your eyes (thoughts) on?

_____

_____

_____

Worship, praise, thankfulness, bearing with someone else's burdens,
fulfilling a need of someone other than yourself: these are all purposes placed in us before we were born (Ephesians 2:10). What is a
purpose you sense God calling you to?

_____

_____

_____

Read Philippians 4: 6-7 (in the margin of the poem). How does
prayer with *"thanksgiving"* help us to receive the *"the peace of God that
transcends all understanding"*?

_____

_____

_____

SURVIVIAL TIP: To suffocate anxiety and fear, count your blessings
and worship. You can't get out of a whole by continuing to dig. When
we worship, we step out...not to mention it freaks out the enemy.

# *Confession*

Ne'er He shall foolishness bless
Break bonds sins possess
Poison taste, spit it out
Healing now as you confess.[59]

[59] Therefore confess your sins to each other and pray for each other so that you may be healed. The prayer of a righteous person is powerful and effective. (James 5:16)

# The Trail Guide: CONFESSION

The cape buffalo is one of the most dangerous animals in Africa, killing approximately 200 people annually. They are fierce. However, lions know best how to hunt this big prey (a bull can weigh up to 1.5 tons). They must first carve him from the herd.

Satan also knows best how to attack us. He operates best in the dark: isolation, shame, guilt, depression. Then, as we go silent, we repeatedly receive his poisonous counsel in the form of lies and deceit- and he goes in for the kill. Whether that is more sin, striking out against others or even harming ourselves, his words (like *"poisonous darts"* - Ephesians 6:16 ) are intended for one outcome: to destroy (John 10:10).

The good news is God knows this and always has a way out (1 Corinthians 10:13). The first thing we must do is get in the daylight! How do we do this? By literally bringing everything into the light. Whether that is confessing a hurt, an emotion, a sin or just the fact that we feel isolated or alone. The very words can free a heart and healing can begin. Confess a sin that only you and God know of- you can use a code word.

_____

_____

_____

_____

Read John 1:1-7. How do we *"walk in the light"* to be *"continually cleansed from all sin"*?

_____

_____

_____

_____

In an unlikely example of how this can work, the movie *"9 Mile"* features the wrapper "Eminem" facing his greatest enemy in an epic "rap battle". Realizing that his adversary already knows so many horrible things about him, Eminem essentially confesses everything his enemy could use against him. By the time his adversary gets the mic…he's speechless. The fuel, the ammo, the evidence…is already destroyed. It's not enough that Satan knows your sins and your weaknesses, he must convince you of your identity in them. He needs the darkness to do it. The light destroys this secrecy and destroys his case as the "accuser".

Read James 5:16 (in the margin). What are some sins that weigh you down that you want to offload?

_____

_____

_____

_____

TOO MUCH WEIGHT: Don't pack more than you are supposed to carry! Solomon speaks about being exhausted as he holds on to sin and it's weight.

*³ When I kept silent, my bones wasted away through my groaning all day long. ⁴ For day and night your hand was heavy on me; my strength was sapped as in the heat of summer. ⁵ Then I acknowledged my sin to you and did not cover up my iniquity. I said, "I will confess my transgressions to the LORD." And you forgave the guilt of my sin.* (Psalm 32:3–5). Like carrying a two-hundred-pound backpack full of rocks of shame and guilt, it's time to cut it loose and walk in freedom!

SURVIVAL TIP: God built us with a poison monitor- our taste buds. When your tongue (your stomach is the second line of defense) touches something toxic, it rejects it. Like the poison we accept when we don't confess sin, it's not meant for good fuel- spit it out!

CHALLENGE: On a small piece of paper, write down a sin that you still struggle with. Fold it up and put in a jar or can. Confess to Jesus that this sin is too heavy, that it's no longer yours and it belongs to Him. The can belongs to the Lord so you can't dig these back out. If it get's full, burn the contents. Accept His peace.

# *Salvation*

Believe, declare, He Is Lord[60]
Within the heart life restored
Baptize now, it is His way[61]
Death died, heaven roared![62]

[60] If you declare with your mouth, "Jesus is Lord," and believe in your heart that God raised him from the dead, you will be saved. (Rom. 10:9)

[61] Peter replied, "Repent and be baptized, every one of you, in the name of Jesus Christ for the forgiveness of your sins. And you will receive the gift of the Holy Spirit." (Acts 2:38)

[62] I tell you that in the same way there will be more rejoicing in heaven over one sinner who repents than over ninety-nine righteous persons who do not need to repent. (Luke 15:7)

## How To Accept The Gift of Salvation: To Defeat Death
### "THE ROMANS ROAD" TO SALVATION

**SIN BROUGHT DEATH**
*"All have sinned and fallen short of the glory of God"* - Romans 3:23
*"For the wages of sin is death, but the gift of God is eternal life in Christ Jesus our Lord"* - Romans 6:23

**CHRIST DIED FOR OUR SIN/OUR DEATH**
*"God demonstrates His own love for us in this: While we were still sinners, Christ died for us"* - Romans 5:8

**WE ACCEPT HIS GIFT THROUGH CONFESSING AND BELIEVING**
*"If you declare with your mouth, "Jesus is Lord," and beleive in your heart that God raised him from the dead, you will be saved."* Romans 10:9-13

**WE ARE BAPTISED**
*"We were buried therefore with him by baptism into death, in order that, just as Christ was raised from the dead by the glory of the Father, we might too walk in newness of life."* Romans 6:4

## The Trail Guide: SALVATION

Did Jesus really have to die for me? Just how deadly would sin have to be for Jesus to willingly come down from heaven, live a perfect life and then be willing to be rejected, tortured and crucified? The Word tells us that the *"wages of sin is death"* (Romans 6:23). It's almost as if we've earned it, just like wages when you would work for something- an outcome. The difficult truth is "sin" is not just a description, it's personal. **MY SIN, YOUR SIN put Jesus on the cross.** God is a just God and He ultimately punishes sin regardless of where it took place or where it resides. Jesus was just willing to take ALL the sin on Himself. What a gift! But, like all gifts, they must be accepted in order to realize their value. God loves us enough to give us the free will to accept or reject this gift. Why? Because you can't have love without the free will to choose it. Furthermore, this gift wasn't bought with money or a credit card. It is the personal embodiment of all of Himself that He could give. Will you choose to open the most expensive, most valuable gift ever given? Want to know how? I am so glad that scripture cited above (Romans 6:23) doesn't end there but with this: *"but the gift of God is eternal life in Christ Jesus our Lord."*

After a long summer camp of hearing the word of God, a young man was asked, "so what have you learned this summer". His answer inspired the hit song *"Should've Been Me"* (by Citizen Way). The lyrics paint a very personal response to what Jesus did:

> *Should've been me, should've been us - Should've*
> *been there hanging on a cross*
> *All of this shame, all of these scars -Should've*
> *been stains that were never washed*
> *Why do I hide, why do you try -Over and over and over again*

*I guess it just leaves me saying thank God -It*
*leaves me saying thank God, thank God*
*For the Should've been*

Before Jesus took the cross, He asks the Father three times to *"take this cup from me"* (Mathew 26:36-45). He wanted to know if there was any other way. The only answer was the cross- the only way was His sacrifice. There is no other gift ("name") by which we can be saved (Acts 4:12). If there was another way, Jesus would've known-there wasn't.

**HOW TO ACCEPT THE GIFT**: Repeat these words or in your own words: "Lord Jesus, I know my sin put you on the cross. I confess you as my Lord and Savior over my life. I know you died, were buried and then resurrected back to life. I accept your gift- thank you!"

Baptism: Do I have to be baptized? The first time the Gospel (the *"good news"* of Christ's *"victory over death"*. 1 Corinthians 5:1-5) is preached, we hear the question, *"what then shall we do"* (Acts 2:36-39). The answer is the same today as then. When we *"put Christ on in baptism"* we receive more than just the gift of salvation. We share in His victory.

CHALLENGE: Hell was *"prepared for the devil and his angels"* (Matthew 25:41), but man can still choose to be there if he rejects the gift. Our opportunity is to share the gift, that we didn't pay for, to the world. Share what you've accepted and bless someone else (Matthew 28:19)

# Victory

It's a victor's name you share,
'Twas your cross that
Christ did bare[63]
Some things too big to be borne,
To Jesus' feet leave them there[64]

Joy is not your goal to claim,
It was yours when took the name
"Glory" more than ever seen,[65]
Ne'er the word shall
mean the same

Keen eyes to the Son did bear,[66]
Compass of your journey where
You will find the healing tree,[67]
I and others meet you there.

[63] For God so loved the world that he gave his one and only Son, that whoever believes in him shall not perish but have eternal life. (John 3:16)

[64] It is for freedom that Christ has set us free. Stand firm, then, and do not let yourselves be burdened again by a yoke of slavery. (Galatian 5:1)

[65] However, as it is written: "What no eye has seen, what no ear has heard, and what no human mind has conceived— the things God has prepared for those who love Him." (1 Cor. 2:9)

[66] I lift up my eyes to the mountains— where does my help come from? My help comes from the Lord, the Maker of heaven and earth. (Ps. 121:1)

[67] Down the middle of the great street of the city. On each side of the river stood the tree of life, bearing twelve crops of fruit, yielding its fruit every month. And the leaves of the tree are for the healing of the nations. (Rev. 22:2)

# The Trail Guide: VICTORY

I love sports. I have played and watched football, baseball, basketball and many other competitive events just for the sheer exhilaration of striving for "VICTORY". However, when I compare those brief moments to our full life's journey in Christ, the word just doesn't mean the same thing. To truly experience joy means to have victory, but to have victory means we have a foe…and in this life it is sin and the death that comes with it (Romans 6:23). To truly understand victory, we must understand what has been defeated and the price that victory required- the very blood of Jesus. When we accept Christ as our Lord and Savior, our name becomes written in the Book of Life (Revelation 3:5), which means our real home is in heaven. We become an adopted son of the Most High God, an HEIR with CHRIST! (Romans 8:17)

It's been said, "Jesus didn't come to make bad people good, He came to make dead people alive." *"But because of his great love for us, God, who is rich in mercy, made us alive with Christ even when we were dead in transgressions… For it is by grace you have been saved, through faith—and this is not from yourselves, it is the gift of God—not by works, so that no one can boast."* (Ephesians 2:4-5) The truth is we were dead in our sin and now we live…and not just for now, forever.

It was over 2,000 years ago when Jesus said, *"I go to prepare a place for you"* (John 14:3). God created heaven and earth in just six days, having rested the seventh. How amazing could heaven be? *"What no eye has seen, what no ear has heard, and what no human mind has conceived"—the things God has prepared for those who love Him"* (1 Corinthians 2:9)

What do you think heaven may be like?

_____

_____

_____

The shortest scripture in the Bible is, *"Jesus Wept"* (John 11:35). Jesus knew his friend, Lazarus, would already be dead when He went to him. However, Jesus wept right before He raised Lazarus from the grave. Read John 11:10-43 Why do you think Jesus allowed Lazarus to die and then weep just before He raised him back to life?

_____

_____

_____

Read Romans 8:16-17. As an *"heir"*, you get to share in the Father's inheritance. How does being an heir to the Kingdom of God compare to other victories you may have experienced?

_____

_____

_____

CHALLENGE: The best victories are shared: The term *"one another"* is in the bible one hundred times in the New Testament alone. It's clear God expects us to be in fellowship (Heb 10:24). Be a part of a group of believers so you can *"bear with one another"* and continue to develop as a mature believer in Christ!

# Final Thoughts

Your foe is pride—it's deceit,[68]
Haughty spirit can unseat
You from the post which God set,
So entertain not conceit

These words are but mirrors of,
The Word of Truth
penned in Love
Study not this mere man's text,
Seek the Word inspired[69] above

Men will mock, the world will rail;
Life can throw burrs by the bale
Son, walk in Christ, He's The Trail,[70]
The woods are His, you will not fail.[71]

[68] For everything in the world—the lust of the flesh, the lust of the eyes, and the pride of life—comes not from the Father but from the world. (1 John 2:16)

[69] All Scripture is God-breathed and is useful for teaching, rebuking, correcting and training in righteousness, so that the servant of God[a] may be thoroughly equipped for every good work. (2 Tim. 3:16–17)

[70] Jesus answered, "I am the way and the truth and the life. No one comes to the Father except through me." (John 14:6)

[71] Not only so, but we ourselves, who have the first fruits of the Spirit, groan inwardly as we wait eagerly for our adoption to sonship, the redemption of our bodies. For in this hope we were saved. But hope that is seen is no hope at all. Who hopes for what they already have? But if we hope for what we do not yet have, we wait for it patiently. In the same way, the Spirit helps us in our weakness. We do not know what we ought to pray for, but the Spirit himself intercedes for us through wordless groans. And he who searches our hearts knows the mind of the Spirit, because the Spirit intercedes for God's people in accordance with the will of God. And we know that in all things God works for the good of those who love him, who have been called according to his purpose. For those God foreknew he also predestined to be conformed to the image of his Son, that he might be the firstborn among many brothers and sisters. And those he predestined, he also called; those he called, he also justified; those he justified, he also glorified. (Rom. 8:23–30)

## The Trail Guide: FINAL THOUGHTS

In one of my favorite movies ever, *"Jeremiah Johnson"*, the main character leaves civilization to become a mountain man after the war. Later in the story, Jeremiah's friend, Del Gue, warns him about the victories Jeremiah has had against a tribe of Crow Indians as they send one warrior at a time to kill him. Del suggests that maybe Jeremiah should leave the mountains as he explains, "a tribe's greatness is figured on how mighty its enemies be." Del advises, "Maybe you best go down to a town, get out of these mountains." Jeremiah reflects and then replies, "I've been to a town, Del."

Once you have tasted grace, victory and peace through Christ- you are a *"new creation"* (2 Corinthians 5:17). There is no reason to return to an old life. You will make mistakes, but the greatest mistake is forgetting who you are and accepting your old self back- your old, *"dead"* self (Romans 6:1). Remember that as long as we *"walk in the light, we are continually cleansed from ALL sin"* (1 John 1:1-7). How does knowing that *"if we walk in the light, as he is in the light, we have fellowship with one another, and the blood of Jesus, his Son, purifies us from all sin"* (I John 1:7) give perspective on how grace works?

_____

_____

_____

_____

_____

The greatest enemies we will face in this life are sin (in all its forms), fear and death. But in Christ we have victory, and our journey isn't over yet. *"For our struggle is not against flesh and blood, but against the rulers, against the authorities, against the powers of this dark world and against the spiritual forces of evil in the heavenly realms. as our fight is not just against flesh and blood."* (Ephesians 6:12).

In the poem's line "The woods are His" we are reminded that *"all things have been created through Him and for Him"* (Colossians 1:16). How does knowing this give you peace as you walk the woods of this life?

_____

_____

_____

In Romans 8:26-30: We see that even though *"we do not know what to pray for"*, the Holy Spirit will intercede for us and that God *"can use all things to the good of those that love Him and who've been called according to His purposes"*. How could trusting God with everything effect how you live every day?

_____

_____

_____

LIFE CHALLENGE: As a sanctified believer in Christ, your testimony is not just your story- it's Christ's victory in you. God's Holy Spirit has actually taken up residence in you (1 Corinthians 3:16) as a "helper" and "teacher" (John 14:26). Just by sharing your story, your testimony, we will share in Christ's victory (Revelation 12:11).

*"NOW GO SHARE THE TREASURE YOU
HAVE FOUND! (Matthew 28:18-20)"*

# Notes

_____

_____

_____

_____

_____

_____

_____

_____

_____

_____

_____

_____

_____

# A Father's Blessing

I have failed, fallen, and messed up more times than I know. In every word, every admonition, every thought toward you... I just want more for you than my mistakes and the wounds they have caused me and others.

I see in you the magnificence of God's glory, His love, His grace, His mercy, and His giftings.

I pray a blessing upon you. I anoint you with oil in the name of the Father, Son, and the Holy Spirit, and I commit you to almighty God. Although you belong to Him, I will always love you but will not force myself upon you as God has not forced Himself upon me.

*The Lord bless you*
*and keep you;*
*the Lord make his face shine on you*
*and be gracious to you;*
*the Lord turn his face toward you*
*and give you peace.*

—Numbers 6:24–26
The Aaronic Priestly Blessing

All wonder at the tree that reaches
As limb and leaf the sun beseeches
But growing roots, though never seen
anchor the tree when others lean

And like the tree, to grow so grand
you must grow down to understand
As winds buffet the greats to fall
We must grow deep before grow tall

# *About the Author*

I grew up the eldest of four in the piney woods of East Texas hunting, fishing, and seeing God's indelible thumbprint in the character of His creation. Having witnessed the demise of my own family dynamic, I longed to someday father a family that would cling to a legacy of faith. Although I experienced what many would consider success in business and in church leadership, the feeling of inadequacy in sending two sons into the world was gripping. "Busyness" and church identity often took precedence over direct time with my children. The guilt of missing opportunities to speak into my sons really set in when they began leaving home for college.

After the loss of my late wife, Laura, writing became an outlet for seeking God's will in what life would look like next. I began learning more of God's nature as a father as I witnessed firsthand how He provided daily through His word, His creation (people) and His Spirit. Although I couldn't wait to share this wisdom with my sons, they were now men. I wrote *The Trail* because I felt paralyzed that I had not prepared my sons for what was to come. What father truly can? The answer, I learned, was THE Father...the best.

Although guilt, inadequacy, grief and false identity attempted to cloud what were the familiar frames of my life, the Lord began healing and redirecting my path. My goal in writing is to remind men of their true identity in Christ and the liberating truth that our Father "*makes our paths straight*" as we trust in Him (Prov. 3:5) regardless of past failures.

\*\*\*\*\*\*\*\*\*\*\*\*\*\*

Brandon has served as a deacon and pastor and currently serves as an elder with StoneWater Church while also advising several companies and charities. Brandon would find love again in Molly. Having met at *Griefshare* (a bible-based program for those who have lost loved ones) as they both had lost their spouses. Together they founded Many Mansions charity which "exists to provide life giving resources through Christ's Kingdom with a focus on widows, orphans and single moms." He and Molly have five children in their blended family. For twenty years the father of a male-dominated household, he is now the lone male in an all-girl (wife and three girls) home… even the pets are female. Stay tuned.

www.thetrailinthewoods.com

CPSIA information can be obtained
at www.ICGtesting.com
Printed in the USA
BVHW040345011021
617866BV00015B/1150

9 781098 014162